Copyright
© 2025 Shelly Zimbelman Copyright registration pending

All rights reserved.

No part of this publication may be reproduced, stored in a retrieval system, or transmitted in any form or by any means—electronic, mechanical, photocopying, recording, or otherwise—without the prior written permission of the publisher, except in the case of brief quotations used in critical articles or reviews.

This book is based on the author's personal experiences and original reflections. Some themes are inspired by widely accepted grief and spiritual healing practices, but all content—including tables, exercises, and narratives—was uniquely created for this work. Any similarity to other published works is purely coincidental or derived from shared, publicly understood concepts within the field of grief support.

First Edition
ISBN: 979-8-9987454-0-9

Printed in the United States of America

Published by:

Legacy Light Studio, LLC St.

Louis, MO

legacylightstudio.com

Cover design and interior layout by: *Shelly Zimbelman*
For permissions, speaking engagements, or group licensing inquiries, please contact:

shelly@legacylightstudio.com

Legacy Light Studio, LLC © 2025

Dedication

For my dad- Your love

shaped my soul,

Your strength lives on in me,

And your presence is forever etched in the quiet moments,

The strokes of my art, And

the words of this book.

This is for you.

Thank you for everything.

--Shelly

Legacy Light Studio, LLC © 2025

Table of Contents

Introduction
- Why This Book?
- What You Will Gain from This Book

Chapter 1 – The Day Life Changed
- My Personal Experience

Chapter 2 – Grief Is Not Linear
- Common Emotions and First Reactions
- My Personal Experience
- What to Remember
- Reflection Exercises: *Grounding in Your Experiences*

Chapter 3 – Navigating Milestones and Special Days
- Understanding Milestones and Special Days
- My Personal Experience
- What to Remember
- Reflection Exercises: *Navigating Grief Through Experiences*

Chapter 4 – Finding Strength in Memories
- The Power of Memories
- Honoring My Father Through Memory and Creation
- Final Thought
- Reflection Exercises: *Honoring Their Memory Through Creation and Connection*

Chapter 5 – Building a Support System
- Strategies for Support and Connection
- My Personal Experience with Support and Spiritual Connection
- What to Remember
- Reflection Exercises: *Support and Spiritual Connection*

Chapter 6 – Rediscovering Purpose and Moving Forward
- Healing Focuses for Moving Forward
- My Personal Experiences Moving Forward
- What to Remember
- Reflection Exercises: *Moving Forward While Honoring Legacy*

Chapter 7 – Conclusion
- A Letter to the Reader **Acknowledgments**

Resources and Further Reading

About the Author

Legacy Light Studio, LLC © 2025

Introduction: Why This Book?

The journey of writing *Finding Light in Loss* began with the profound experience of losing my father. His passing left a void that felt impossible to fill, and I found myself navigating a landscape of grief that was both unfamiliar and overwhelming. In the midst of this sorrow, I searched for ways to not only process my emotions but also to honor his life and the love we shared. Through that journey, I discovered that healing is not about moving on or forgetting—it is about learning how to carry love forward in a new and meaningful way.

As I walked this path, I realized that so many others were also struggling to find hope in their own losses. Grief can be isolating, and I wanted to offer a source of comfort, understanding, and encouragement to those who felt alone in their pain. Writing *Finding Light in Loss* became my way of reaching out to others, sharing what I had learned, and helping people find peace amidst their sorrow.

This book is not just about loss; it is about resilience, love, and the strength that can emerge from even the deepest heartbreak. It blends personal experiences with practical insights and spiritual wisdom, offering readers a compassionate guide to navigating grief while embracing life's continued beauty. Faith played a significant role in my own healing journey, reminding me that our loved ones remain with us in spirit and that love transcends the boundaries of life and death. Through divine connection, I found reassurance that I was never truly alone and that even in grief, there is a greater purpose unfolding.

My hope is that *Finding Light in Loss* serves as a companion for those who are searching for a way forward, reminding them that even in darkness, there is still light to be found. By embracing both the seen and unseen, we can open our hearts to healing, allowing faith, love, and the presence of those we've lost to guide us toward peace.

Ultimately, I wrote this book to let others know they are not alone. Grief is a journey, but it does not have to be walked in solitude. By sharing our stories and supporting one another, we can transform loss into a powerful force for love, connection, and spiritual healing. A little warning upfront, my story is an intense week of very detailed emotional roller coasters.

Legacy Light Studio, LLC © 2025

What You'll Gain from This Book:

- **Emotional Support and Understanding**
  A compassionate voice that validates your grief and offers comfort through shared experience.
- **Spiritual Insight and Encouragement**
  Reflections on faith, love, and the soul's journey that bring peace and perspective during difficult times.
- **Practical Tools for Healing**
  Gentle guidance on processing grief, building a support system, and creating space for self-care.
- **Ways to Honor and Remember**
  Ideas for keeping your father's memory alive while allowing yourself to live with meaning and purpose.
- **Empowerment to Move Forward**
  Encouragement to step into a life of love, resilience, and renewed hope—without guilt.
- **A Deeper Connection to Love**
  A reminder that love never dies; it evolves, guiding you as you walk forward with an open heart.

Legacy Light Studio, LLC © 2025

CHAPTER 1 - THE DAY LIFE CHANGED

My personal experience of loss

October 31, 2022, started like any other day. It was a crisp autumn morning, the kind where the chill in the air hinted at the approaching winter. I was off work, enjoying the rare opportunity to take things slow. Then, around 10:00 AM, my phone buzzed.

It was a text from my mom. *"Come to the hospital."* This text started a weeklong ordeal, involving four hospitals.

She didn't say much else, just that my dad wasn't feeling well, that he had been taken to a hospital an hour and a half away from where I live. My heart started pounding. I scrambled to make sense of what was happening.

Earlier that morning, around 5:00 AM, my dad had woken up with chest pressure. He didn't tell my mom. Maybe he didn't want to worry her, or maybe he thought it would pass. It wasn't until 8:30 in the morning, that he finally admitted something was wrong. She convinced him to go to the doctor, but in true Dad fashion, he drove himself.

By 9:00 AM, he was at his local physician's office, where they performed an ECG (an electrocardiogram of his heart rhythm). The results were concerning—so much so that they told him he needed to go straight to the emergency room. He still didn't ask for help. He drove himself there, completely unaware that his body was already slipping into cardiogenic shock (a life-threatening condition where the heart muscles are not working, and the heart cannot pump enough blood to the needs of the body).

Meanwhile, at work, my mom got the call. The hospital wasn't equipped to handle his condition, so they were transferring him to another hospital 30 minutes away. That was when she sent me the text.

I didn't hesitate. I called my job to let them know I had to go. Then I called my husband. My hands were shaking as I frantically packed a bag, trying to prepare for the unknown. I was headed to the garage, ready to leave, when my phone rang again, it was my mom. *Hold off,* she said. *They might transfer him to St. Louis instead.*

That stopped me in my tracks. I lived in the St. Louis area, so if he was being moved there, I wouldn't need to rush just yet. I waited anxiously. Minutes felt like hours. Then another call—he was still going one town over to a slightly larger hospital, for now, 30 minutes from where they live. I grabbed my keys and drove.

By the time I arrived at the hospital, dad hadn't gotten there yet. Mom was still at home, waiting for the first hospital to let her know when he would be transferred. My nephew had arrived at the hospital where they were transferring him first, and together, we made the 30-minute drive to pick her up so she would not have to drive herself.

When we returned to the 2nd hospital, Dad was finally there. He was sitting up, talking. His breathing was labored, but his spirit was strong—he was even cracking jokes, as if nothing serious was happening. Six hours. That's how long it took the first hospital to transfer him. Six hours that could have changed everything.

This hospital was bigger than the smaller hospital where my parents live but was not fully equipped to handle multiple cardiac emergencies at once. They only had one cardiologist on duty, and there were multiple patients with serious heart conditions. He was put on a waiting list for a cath lab procedure (where they use x-ray to look at the blood vessels in the heart), but for the moment, he seemed stable. My mom, nephew, and I decided to step out for a quick dinner, figuring we had some time.

We never even got our food.

Before it arrived, we received a call—Dad was already in the cath lab. We rushed back to the hospital, our hearts pounding with fear and uncertainty. A recurring theme throughout the week. In that waiting room, time stood still. Then, the doctor walked in.

His words shattered everything.

Only **10% of my dad's heart muscle** was functioning. Every artery was nearly **100% blocked**. He needed immediate intervention to survive.
The doctor looked at us, his expression grave but determined. He explained that they needed permission to try to open up the two main arteries on both sides of his heart. There was no choice. If they didn't try, he wouldn't make it.

And flying him to St. Louis? Not an option. If they put him on a helicopter in his condition, he wouldn't survive the flight.

There was no hesitation.

"Do whatever you have to do."
And with that, they rushed back in to try and save him.

The Weight of Waiting

We were all gathered in the waiting room when the doctor gave us the devastating news. My dad's heart was failing—only **10% of it was functioning**, and every artery was nearly **100% blocked**. Despite it all, the doctor told us, Dad was **alert and talking up a storm** in true Dad fashion. Even in crisis, he was still himself.

As soon as the doctor left, the weight of reality crashed down on me. I couldn't sit still. I walked out into the hallway, barely able to breathe, my hands shaking as I pulled out my phone. The first person I called was my aunt—my mom's sister. As soon as she answered, I broke down. Hysterical sobs racked my body as I tried to explain what was happening. She didn't hesitate. She immediately started calling my other aunts and cousins, and within minutes, they were on the road, making the two-hour drive to be with us.

Next, I called my husband, who was still at work. My voice cracked as I tried to keep it together, but there was no holding back the fear in my voice. After that, I dialed my daughter. She was in Atlanta at the time, on an externship for her college degree. The thought of telling her over the phone, from so far away, was unbearable.

But by some stroke of luck—or maybe fate—her boyfriend was there visiting. He had a flight scheduled for the next day, and without hesitation, she booked a seat on the same plane. She was coming home.

Inside the waiting room, emotions ran high. My sister, who had arrived earlier in the evening, was crying uncontrollably. My mom sat beside her, her face wet with tears, her hands clasped tightly together as she prayed. I could feel the weight of it all—the fear, the helplessness, the desperate hope that somehow, against all odds, my dad would pull through.

As I was reaching out to my mom's side of the family, my sister was calling my dad's. His two brothers immediately left to come to the hospital and arrived before the procedure was even finished. By the time the doctors completed the cath lab procedure, my aunts and cousins had also arrived. The waiting room, once too big and too quiet, was now full of family, each of us clinging to the only thing we had at that moment: each other.

A Glimmer of Hope

Time in the waiting room felt endless. Every second stretched unbearably as we sat there, consumed by fear, whispering prayers, and bracing ourselves for the worst. Then, finally, the doctor returned with an update.

He had done it.
He was able to **open the two main arteries**, restoring some of the blood flow to my dad's failing heart. As he spoke, I felt the first flicker of relief, though it was fragile and uncertain. The doctor explained that they had placed a **temporary circulation pump** in his right

femoral artery in his leg to help his heart function. It was a step forward, but we weren't out of danger yet.

Shortly after, they wheeled him out to the ICU (intensive care unit) to recover. Seeing him at that moment—hooked up to machines, fragile yet still fighting—was overwhelming. We were only able to visit briefly, but in those few minutes, just knowing he had made it through the procedure, gave us hope.

We weren't allowed to stay overnight, so reluctantly, we made the **30-minute drive back to my mom's house** for the night. One of my aunts and a cousin stayed with us, wanting to be close. My sister, emotionally drained, decided to go back home two hours away.

As I lay in bed that night, exhaustion pressed down on me, but sleep wouldn't come. My mind raced with worry, questions, and prayers. **Would he make it through the night? Would tomorrow bring better news—or more devastation?**

All we could do was wait.

The Call That Changed Everything

At sunrise, my mom's phone rang. It was the cardiologist.

My mom was still reeling from the night before—emotionally drained, barely holding herself together. When she saw who was calling, she shook her head, her eyes already welling with tears. *"I can't,"* she whispered, pushing the phone toward me.

So, I stepped out onto the deck and answered.

The cardiologist's voice was calm but serious. He explained that while my dad had survived the procedure, the hospital simply **wasn't equipped** to provide the level of care he needed. His condition was fragile, and there were growing concerns about his kidneys and other organs.

"He needs to be at a hospital with a full team of specialists," he said. *"I recommend transferring him as soon as possible."*
I didn't hesitate. *"Yes, please—transfer him."*

The plan was set Dad would be flown to a **hospital in St. Louis** for the critical care he needed.

When I stepped back inside to tell my mom, panic set in.

She didn't care about packing a bag. She didn't care about preparing her dog for the trip to my house. She just wanted to **go**—right then, straight to the hospital, before they put him on that helicopter.

Her voice trembled as she pleaded with me. *"Why can't we just go now? We can come back for everything later!"*

I tried to reason with her. I wanted her to take a moment, to breathe, to prepare for the long road ahead. But I could see it in her eyes—logic wasn't going to win this battle. My own emotions surged, and all I could do was nod. *"We can."*

Without another word, we all rushed to the car, making the **thirty-minute drive** back to the hospital, desperate to see him before he was flown out.

When we arrived, we learned that the helicopter **wasn't even there yet**, it was out on another trip. More waiting. More uncertainty.

After back-and-forth discussions with the medical team, they confirmed **Air Evac** would handle the transfer. But I made the difficult choice to leave before the helicopter arrived.

I turned to my mom. *"I'm going back to your house to get the dog and drive to St. Louis,"* I told her. I needed to make sure everything was settled, so when she arrived, she wouldn't have to worry about anything but Dad.

She refused to leave until she saw him get on that helicopter. So, as I drove away, she stayed behind, waiting—watching the sky for the flight that would carry him toward the care he desperately needed.

So, while my **mom, aunts, and cousins stood there, watching as Dad was loaded onto the stretcher and lifted into the air**, I was already on the highway. And then, as I glanced up at the sky, I saw it.

The helicopter.

It was a surreal moment—knowing that my dad was inside, flying toward life-saving care, while I was on the road, racing to meet him there.

Meanwhile, my daughter was also **in the air**, on a flight home from Atlanta, set to land around the same time I would be back in St. Louis.

The roller coaster's just kept going, on an endless ride, with emotional turmoil at every twist and turn.

While I was arriving back in St. Louis, and after the helicopter had left with my dad in tow, my aunt took my mom back to her house to finally pack a bag. I settled the dog at home, then immediately headed to the airport to pick up my daughter. The moment she stepped off the plane, I felt a wave of relief seeing her. But there was no time to process it—we hugged, got in the car, and drove **straight to the hospital in St. Louis**, where Dad was now fighting for his life.

Stay with me... I know this story is a lot to keep reading.

The Third Hospital: Holding On and Another Transfer

By the time I arrived at the third hospital, it was around **3 in the afternoon**. Dad was in a private room on the **cardiac floor**, hooked up to every machine they had—each one working at **maximum capacity**. I watched the monitors, the endless beeping filling the space, and I overheard the nurses whispering to each other.

"Maybe the levels are reading correctly... because that's what's happening." That sentence stuck with me. They were seeing it unfold in real-time.

An hour later, my mom and aunts arrived. Despite everything, **Dad was talking**—fully aware, completely lucid. He even wanted to talk to his brother, so we called him, and they spoke over the phone.

At one point during the conversation, Dad said something that sent a chill through me.

"I might be getting to see Jesus soon."

The room was big enough for family to gather, with some sitting on the couch, others in chairs scattered around. But **not everyone could stay in the room for long**. My sister and mom spent a lot of time in the waiting room—**it was too hard for my sister to see Dad like this**. She just couldn't bear to watch him slipping away.

When the doctor finally came in, he confirmed what the nurses had been saying—Dad was **maxed out on everything**. The machines were doing all they could. The only remaining option was an **LVAD (Left Ventricular Assist Device)**—a mechanical pump that could help his failing heart.

But there was a problem. (another curve on the roller coaster)

That procedure couldn't be done here. They didn't have the capability. The only hospital that could evaluate him for it was located in St. Louis and was a top ten hospital.

And yet- another problem, there wasn't a **bed available** in their **cardiac ICU**. So, we had to wait.

That night, my **husband arrived after work**. Seeing how exhausted we all were, he volunteered to **stay overnight with Dad** so my mom, my daughter, and I could finally go to my house to sleep. Everyone else went back to their own homes, needing rest after the emotional rollercoaster of the last two days.

But **sleep didn't last long**.

At **2 in the morning**, my phone rang. It was my husband.

"They're transferring him."

We barely had time to process it. Just like that, Dad was being flown **across the city**—his **fourth and final hospital transfer**.

Exhausted but running on pure adrenaline, we got up, threw on whatever clothes were closest, and **rushed to this last hospital.**

It had now been **only two and a half days** since this whole nightmare began—but it felt like a lifetime.

Final Hospital: Searching for Hope

This hospital was **huge**. After parking and walking **what felt like forever**, we finally found the correct elevator and made our way up to the **10th floor**.

When we arrived, they let us in **only briefly,** before telling us that only **one person** could stay overnight in the room with Dad. The waiting room wasn't designed for overnight stays, the **chairs didn't recline**, and there was **nowhere comfortable to sleep**.

So, we did what we could. My mom, my daughter, and I tried to push some chairs together, creating **a makeshift bed**, but it didn't do much. **None of us really slept.**

Meanwhile, my husband stayed **in the room with Dad**—keeping watch, making sure he wasn't alone.

By the time **morning came—Wednesday, Day 3**—we were running on empty. At **7 AM**, they finally allowed us back into his room.

And there he was—**still talking.**

Even hooked up to all sorts of **machines**, with a **morphine drip running since Monday**, he was still cracking jokes and keeping up with conversations. Seeing him alert made it feel, for a moment, like **maybe things were okay**.

That hope grew when we met his **amazing nurse**, who took the time to **explain everything in detail**. For the first time in days, it felt like we had a **real chance**. But that glimmer of hope **faded** when the medical team came in.

Dad was **incredibly critical**. His heart had suffered too much damage, and with **his age and the severity of his condition**, they weren't sure he would **qualify for the LVAD procedure**.

The news hit like a gut punch. (when would this ride ever stop!)

We had fought so hard to get him here—to this hospital, to these specialists—only to hear that **he might not even be a candidate** for the one thing that could **save his life.**

The room felt heavy with silence after the doctors left. None of us knew what to say. Dad, though, broke the tension with a small smile. "Well, I guess that means I just have to prove them wrong, huh?"

He always had a way of making the unbearable a little lighter. But beneath his humor, I could see the exhaustion in his eyes.

We spent the rest of the morning by his side, listening to his stories—some old, some new. He talked about my childhood, about my daughter, about all the things he still wanted to do. It was as if he was making sure we carried every piece of him with us, no matter what happened next.

For the remainder of the morning, Dad spent a lot of quality time with each of us. A monitor in the room displayed relaxation scenes, gentle landscapes and peaceful nature visuals. We played soothing music, and to my surprise, Dad kept singing "Jesus Loves Me." It struck me as odd that he chose a children's song, but he was genuinely happy. In fact, he never displayed anything but joy during this last week of his life.

Throughout the day, no doctors came, only the nurse who cared for him with such patience and kindness. My cousin was with us every minute, providing support and sharing in the quiet moments.

Dad spent a lot of time talking about paintings he wanted to create. He was a truly talented artist, and even in these moments, his mind was still full of creativity. He described colors, brushstrokes, and the images he saw in his mind. It was as if he was still dreaming, still planning, still holding onto the beauty he wanted to bring into the world.

Things took a bit of a turn after shift change that evening. The night nurse was more about business and not as friendly. She let us know to keep quieter. She wasn't wrong, we were a bit loud for the environment of a cardiac ICU.

That evening, my husband attempted to take me home for some rest. My mother wouldn't leave, so she and my cousin stayed in that really uncomfortable waiting room. Emotionally drained, my husband and I had just arrived home and were attempting to take a minute on our deck when we got a call from my mother: "Don't go to bed." So, we went back to the hospital once again. During this entire week none of us slept. We averaged a couple of hours each night.

Legacy Light Studio, LLC © 2025

When were back at the hospital, a doctor came to talk to us about Dad. She was probably the best doctor we saw that week.

They had performed a CT (computed tomography) scan of Dad's chest, abdomen, and pelvis. She explained that his lungs were full of disease, his heart appeared enlarged, but the most concerning thing was an abscessed kidney stone that had been tucked behind his kidney.

Dad had a history of kidney stones, so he probably didn't think much of any pain he might have been experiencing from that stone. The doctor told us that while there was no way to know for sure, the abscessed stone could have caused the heart attack because of the infection spread—or it could have been the other way around, with the heart attack leading to the abscess formation and infection.

Regardless, he needed immediate surgery to remove the abscess and infection.

Late Wednesday night, Dad went to surgery. For the first time, he expressed concern about being intubated. He was afraid he would never come off the ventilator.

Going into Thursday, we learned that they had successfully removed the abscess and the pump in Dad's leg. Apparently, the pump had not been put in correctly, and this hospital was critical of the skill of the previous hospital that had placed it. Did it even matter at this point?

When I walked into his room and saw him lying there, silent, with the ventilator breathing for him, it felt like the air had been stolen from my own lungs. My dad—my strong, stubborn, full-of-life dad—was still, his chest rising and falling in time with the machine. It was a sight that shattered me.

My husband squeezed my hand, grounding me in that moment, reminding me that we weren't giving up hope. Not yet, while he whispered, "it's ok sweety, he just looks that way, because he just came out of surgery, it's temporary".

Hours passed in slow motion, each second feeling heavier than the last. And then, finally, they removed the ventilator.

I held my breath, waiting.

Then, like a miracle, his eyes opened. A slow, groggy smile spread across his face. "Well, that was fun," he croaked, his voice scratchy but unmistakably his.
Laughter mixed with relieved tears. He was still here. He was still fighting.

He cracked jokes, his wit untouched by the trauma his body had endured. The room, once suffocating with worry, filled with warmth again. For a little while, it felt like we had him back.

The medications kept his blood circulating, keeping him with us just a little longer. We clung to that time, to every word, to every moment. But deep down, we knew—we were still standing at the edge of an uphill battle.

Thursday was filled with emotion. My sister, nephew, and brother-in-law were trying to work and come to the hospital when they could. Emotions ran high. My sister couldn't bring herself to sit by Dad's side and touch him. She had a breakdown in the waiting room, and my mom consoled her. Mom and I had a meltdown, exchanging harsh words in the weight of it all. My daughter broke down, sobbing that her grandpa would never get to know her future kids.

And yet, through it all, Dad remained in good spirits. He kept talking to us, making jokes, and laughing. But one thing bothered him—he hated the curtain in his room. His bed faced it directly, and he kept complaining about how ugly it was.

And no matter how much we begged, my mom refused to go rest in the hotel room. Dad kept telling her to go, insisting she needed to take care of herself. But she wouldn't leave his side. He was more concerned about her than himself.

Despite the brief moments of relief and laughter with Dad, Thursday also brought more stress and frustration.

At some point in the day, a first-year resident doctor walked into the room, his words as cold as they were abrupt. Without any warning, without even the smallest ounce of compassion, he bluntly stated, "If you take him off his medication, he will die." (We get it, Ok!)

The words hit like a slap. There was no explanation, no preparation, just a statement of brutal finality. My mom and I just stared at him, caught between shock and anger. How could he say something like that so casually? How could he not see that we were already drowning in fear, clinging to whatever hope we had left?

And then, later, as I walked down the hall, a nurse stopped me. I expected some reassurance, some kindness, but instead, her words cut just as deep. In a sharp, almost condescending tone, she informed me that the only people who had any say in Dad's care were him and my mom.

I stood there for a moment, stunned. Where was this coming from? No one was trying to override decisions or make demands—we were just a family, standing together, trying to support the man we loved. It was one of those moments where I wished all people in the medical field understood that words matter. Delivery matters. Compassion matters.

My husband, who had been my rock through all of this, had finally had enough. He pulled the resident doctor aside and gave him a firm, no-nonsense, "come-to-Jesus" talk about bedside manner. In no uncertain terms, he let him know just how inappropriate their behavior had been. That you don't just walk into a room and drop devastating news like it's a clinical note. That families—people—deserve better than that.

Legacy Light Studio, LLC © 2025

And in that moment, I was so grateful for my husband. For his strength. For his ability to speak up when I felt too exhausted to fight one more battle.

Friday: Holding On

Friday morning started much the same as the day before. No drastic changes, no new information—just the slow, steady march of uncertainty. The exhaustion had fully set in, but there was no time to rest.

Thursday night, I had gone home for a few hours of sleep, but it hadn't done much to ease the emotional weight pressing down on me. When I returned to the hospital early Friday morning, Dad was awake and alert, talking with all of us. He seemed content in these moments, still joking, still present. We spent as much time as we could just sitting with him, listening to his voice, memorizing his face, holding onto whatever time we had left.

At one point in the day, a doctor came in and spoke with us. He reassured my mom that they were monitoring everything and working through things step by step. He didn't offer promises, but he didn't take away hope either. And for my mom, that was enough. She clung to his words like a lifeline, holding on to the idea that maybe, just maybe, we still had a path forward.

But the small comfort of that moment didn't last.

Later in the evening, the medical team came rushing in with urgency. Dad's blood flow had started clotting off to his right arm, and if they didn't intervene immediately, he would lose it. There was no choice—he had to go back into surgery.

Everything became a blur again. Another procedure. Another unknown. Another moment of standing in a hospital hallway, watching helplessly as they wheeled him away.

Before and after the surgery, one thing became clear—Dad was unbearably thirsty. He couldn't drink, but he constantly begged us to use the long Q-tip-shaped swabs to wet his lips. He asked for the small, wet sponges meant to soothe his dry mouth, and he wanted them almost constantly. His right arm was too weak to lift, so he relied on us. We all took turns—dipping the swabs, pressing them gently to his lips, trying to bring him some small relief. He was demanding about it, asking again and again. It was one of the few things he had control over, and we did everything we could to make him comfortable.

But as the night wore on, something changed.

The hallucinations became stronger. That awful curtain—the one he had hated since the moment he'd arrived—was coming alive in his mind. He saw things there that we couldn't see. At first, it was small, but as time passed, he became more and more convinced that what he saw was real.

And all we could do was sit beside him, hold his hand, and keep going. Because at that point, it was all we had left to give.

Friday Night and Saturday

Friday night, we finally convinced Mom to go to the hotel to get some rest. Family members had been coming and going all week, but she hadn't left Dad's side for a moment. My daughter and one of my nephews went with her to ensure she got some sleep, while my husband stayed in the hospital room with Dad.

Around 5 AM, my phone rang. It was my husband. "The doctors want to have a family meeting first thing this morning. You all need to come now."

We jumped out of bed, threw on clothes, and rushed back to the hospital. Mom, exhausted and barely functioning, resisted at first—she didn't want to be rushed. But we knew we had to get her there. My nephew found a wheelchair and gently convinced her to let him push her across the long walk to the hospital.

When we arrived, Mom's first words to my husband were, "Just tell me. Is he dead?"

He wasn't. But something had shifted.

We went into Dad's room, and the moment Mom walked in, he looked at her and said, "You have to let me go."

Mom broke down. She shook her head, her voice rising with grief. "You promised me you would try!" She turned away, sobbing in the corner of the room. The rest of us gathered around Dad, holding his hands, whispering to him that it was okay. That we loved him. That he didn't have to fight anymore.

And then, just as quickly, he was laughing. Telling jokes. As if the weight of the moment had never happened. As if he wanted to shield us from the inevitable.

Mom couldn't take it. It was too much, too soon.

The doctor on duty finally spoke. "Okay. Here's what we're going to do."
Dad had made his wishes clear, and we all thought we knew what would come next. We left Mom and Dad alone for some time together.

Then shift change happened. Hours passed. Nothing happened.

We waited. But the nurses weren't disconnecting any medications. It was as if no one was listening to Dad's wishes.

Confusion turned into frustration.

Then, a nurse coldly informed my husband and me, "Your dad changed his mind. It's not up to the rest of you."

We were stunned. None of us had known that behind closed doors, Mom had spoken with Dad—and he had decided to keep fighting.

Saturday felt different.

Dad had one last surgery that day, a procedure to cut open his calves to relieve the pressure from the blood pooling in his legs. At this point, the surgeries felt endless, each one an attempt to buy just a little more time, a little more hope. But something about this day felt final, even if none of us wanted to say it out loud.

When he returned from surgery, something shifted. He was more present, more aware than he had been all week. It was as if he knew—this was his last chance to say everything he needed to say.

One by one, he had deep, personal conversations with each of us. Real conversations. The kind that stay with you forever.

To my daughter, he was firm but loving: "Finish school. No matter what, you finish." He told her over and over how proud he was of her; how much he believed in her. And then, in a moment that surprised us all, he told her that he approved of her boyfriend. He had never outright said it before, but that day, he made sure she knew. (That boyfriend is now her fiancé, by the way.)

When it was my turn, I sat by his bed, struggling to find the right words. Finally, I just said the simplest, truest thing I could: "I'm going to miss talking to you."
He looked at me with those familiar eyes, full of love and wisdom, and I knew he already understood.

Then, after a long pause, he chuckled softly and said, "I sure am talking a lot, aren't I? It isn't like me, is it?"

We all laughed through the tears because he was right—he was talking more than he ever had. It was as if he was trying to fit a lifetime of conversations into this one day. And we hung onto every word.

That night, my oldest nephew stayed with him in the hospital room. My mom and I, for the first time in what felt like forever, stayed in the hotel room. It felt wrong to be away from him, but we also knew we needed rest.

Even in those final moments, he was still teaching us things—about love, about strength, about how to say goodbye even when you don't want to.

Legacy Light Studio, LLC © 2025

Going into Sunday, we returned to the hospital first thing in the morning. Mom went in alone at first. When I joined her, she was hugging Dad, then turned to me, her eyes full of something I hadn't seen in days—peace. "It's okay, I am okay," she said softly.

She then told me that Dad had spoken to Jesus all night. He told her that Jesus had said he wasn't going to heal his body here—he was taking him home. That knowledge gave Mom a sense of peace she hadn't yet found in this nightmare.

I hugged her, then turned to Dad, whispering that I loved him. Mom asked me to gather the family, so one by one, we all came—my sister, brother-in-law, nephews, daughter, husband, cousin, and the doctor.

The doctor explained in detail what Dad's future would look like if he continued treatment—permanent dialysis, a ventilator, medications that would never stop circulating his blood, and a life bound to machines, unable to function on his own.

Dad listened carefully; then firmly said he didn't want that. When asked when he wanted to begin the process of letting go, he simply waved his hand—right now.

The doctor's eyes glistened with unshed tears. My husband, standing behind me, was crying so hard he nearly knocked me over as he held me tight.

I felt something unexpected—relief. Relief that Dad wouldn't suffer anymore. That his pain would finally end. Around me, the room was filled with sobs, yet Mom didn't cry. Instead, she held onto the peace that Dad had given her that morning, knowing he was ready.

My sister had to leave the room. She was always Dad's little girl, and the weight of the moment was too much. But Dad understood—he always did.

One by one, they disconnected the medications and machines, and yet, he remained alert, talking with us all throughout the day. It was nothing short of astonishing. He was present, engaged, sharing memories, laughter, and wisdom, holding on with a strength that left us all in awe.

At one point, he began planning his funeral with us—not in sorrow, but with a sense of acceptance and even humor. He told us exactly what he wanted: the style of his coffin, the details of his military honors, the words that should be etched into his headstone. He made sure we knew which of his belongings should go to each of us, dividing them with care and intention, making sure we would each have something to hold onto. It was heartbreaking and beautiful all at once.

At 3 PM, his preacher arrived. We gave Dad, Mom, and the preacher some time alone. I wasn't sure what was being said in that quiet space, but when I walked in, Mom turned to me, her eyes filled with something that looked like peace.

"You have to hear what your dad has told us," She said.

Legacy Light Studio, LLC © 2025

And then, Dad looked at me and shared something so incredible, so profound, that I knew this moment would stay with me forever.

I stood at the foot of his bed, watching him intently. Dad locked eyes with me; his gaze unwavering, full of something I couldn't quite explain. Then, with slow, deliberate movements, he began to speak.

"I was talking to Jesus all night," he said, his voice steady. His hands moved as he spoke, illustrating his words. "I kept going up," he said, raising both arms high above his head, "through a tunnel with all of these other souls." Then, he brought his hands back down. "And I kept coming back down," he repeated, moving his arms up and down, over and over again, as if reliving the experience in real-time.

"Each time, I was standing outside this gate, and Jesus was there. And He told me, 'Go back. Your work is not finished yet.'"

I was completely still, absorbing every word. Later, my nephew would tell me that Dad had indeed been talking to someone all night—conversing in a way that made it clear he wasn't alone in that room.

After Dad finished telling me his experience, the preacher, who had been sitting nearby, shook his head in quiet awe. He had spent forty years by the bedsides of the dying, but he had never witnessed anything like this. "I will never forget this," he said, visibly moved. Neither would I. None of us would.

After the preacher left, Dad whispered personal messages into each of our ears—words meant only for us. I don't know what he said to the others, but I knew, without a doubt, that whatever it was, it mattered.

He remained lucid until just a few hours before he passed. Until about three hours before the end, he still recognized me. But in that final hour, there was only one voice that reached him—Mom's. Over and over again, he responded to her voice alone, telling her repeatedly, "I love you."

As I sit here, recounting the details of this week, I do this with a determination to share with each of you the very real trauma that comes with the moments that lead up to and surround the death of a loved one. Your experience may or may not have been as much of a roller coaster as mine, but the one thing I know, is that love is what got me through it all. And love is what we all have to find – love for ourselves, love for our loved ones, and love for the very life that each of us has been given the opportunity to experience.

In those final days, I felt an overwhelming, unexplainable joy radiating from my dad. It was as though the very air in the room was infused with pure, undiluted love. Despite the grim reality of death looming near, there was a sense of lightness, a palpable joy that enveloped everyone present. It was as if time stood still, and for a fleeting moment, the sorrow of loss gave way to something far greater—something that filled the room with peace.

That moment—when I felt his love more than ever before—was transformative. It wasn't just about him, or about the pain of his inevitable passing; it was about the profound truth that love is boundless. It transcends the physical world, and it never truly leaves us. My father's love was not just an echo in that room—it was a call to something bigger, a mission that could no longer be ignored.

I knew, deep in my soul, that my destiny was clear. I was meant to carry this message forward: that love is not just a fleeting emotion, but a force that runs through all of us, in all things. And just as his love filled the room in his last moments, I now feel compelled to spread that same joy and love to others. My journey is to ignite hearts with the truth that we are all capable of this love—radiant, powerful, and eternal.

The remaining chapters of this book are designed for you to think about your grief, understand the layered processes of grief, hear how I handled my grief, and reflect on your own path through your grief. None of us are alone as we wade through the trenches of losing a loved one.

Legacy Light Studio, LLC © 2025

CHAPTER 2 - GRIEF IS NOT LINEAR

COMMON EMOTIONS AND FIRST REACTION

Losing a father is a life-altering event, and the emotions that follow can feel overwhelming, unpredictable, and even confusing. Everyone experiences grief differently, but there are common reactions that many people go through. Understanding these emotions—and knowing that they are natural—can help you process your loss in a healthy way.

Below are some common stages of grief, and suggestions for dealing with each stage. It was helpful to me to learn about these stages, and I actually practiced some of these things, like journaling. I hope you find it just as helpful—and that it reminds you that whatever you're feeling right now, you are not alone."

Grief Stage	*Common Experiences*	*Practical Coping Suggestions*	*Spiritual Perspective*
Shock and Numbness	Feeling emotionally numb, detached, or as if the world has stopped.	Talk to a trusted friend or counselor, allow yourself to rest, and give yourself permission to feel numb.	Lean on prayer, scripture, or meditation to trust in a greater plan.
Denial and Disbelief	Difficulty accepting the reality of the loss, thinking it can't be true.	Write down your thoughts in a journal, engage in grounding activities, and gently remind yourself of reality through routines.	Remind yourself the soul continues beyond physical death.
Overwhelming Sadness and Loneliness	Profound sadness, sense of identity loss, and loneliness.	Connect with a support group, express emotions through creative outlets, or schedule regular check-ins with loved ones.	Look for signs of their presence; stay connected through prayer or meditation.
Guilt and Regret	Struggles with 'what if' thoughts and regrets over unresolved issues.	Write a letter to your father expressing your feelings, speak to a therapist, or engage in self-compassion exercises.	Seek forgiveness through spiritual rituals or write a letter to your loved one.
Anger and Frustration	Anger at circumstances, others, or even the person who passed away.	Channel anger through physical activity like walking or exercise, or express it through journaling or art.	Turn to faith or spiritual mentors to find deeper understanding and surrender anger.
Fear and Anxiety	Uncertainty about the future, feeling unsupported or vulnerable.	Create a daily routine, break tasks into manageable steps, and talk through your fears with someone you trust.	Affirm that divine or spiritual support is still with you; repeat comforting prayers.
Physical Symptoms of Grief	Fatigue, appetite changes, sleep disturbances, and physical tension.	Maintain a healthy routine, get light exercise, eat balanced meals, and consider seeing a healthcare provider if symptoms persist.	Use spiritual practices like meditation, prayer, or nature walks to support healing.

This table was developed from personal experience and spiritual reflection, inspired by widely recognized grief models such as the Five Stages of Grief introduced by Elisabeth Kübler-Ross. For additional psychological frameworks, see: Kübler-Ross, E., & Kessler, D. (2005). On Grief and Grieving: Finding the Meaning of Grief Through the Five Stages of Loss. Scribner.

My Personal Experience

In the immediate days following my father's death, I moved through life in a haze of responsibility and numbness. I stayed close to my mother, helping her with funeral arrangements and military benefits, trying to be her rock while burying my own emotions. I poured myself into writing his eulogy, which I also delivered—a way to hold myself together when everything inside me felt like it was unraveling. This was my initial shock and numbness stage.

After the funeral, I returned to work and focused intensely on tasks, shielding myself from conversations about his death. I couldn't allow myself to talk about it—not yet. The grief was too raw, and I feared that if I let it out, it would consume me. At home, life resumed its rhythm, but I was quietly breaking. I didn't want to talk about it all the time, even though it lived under the surface of every moment.

In those first few months, I had vivid dreams where I saw my dad—sometimes we talked, and other times I simply heard him call my name. These moments felt like spiritual bridges, reminding me that love and connection continue beyond the physical. They deepened my sense of purpose and awakened something inside me that I'm only now beginning to understand fully.

Grief lived quietly within me. I cried alone on many days, letting the tears fall only when no one was watching. I was the strong one for everyone else, the steady hand in the storm—but inside, I was changed. Irrevocably so.

In some ways, I will never be the same again. But I've learned that healing doesn't mean returning to who you were. It means learning to move forward with grace, carrying love in a new way. Some days, the only thing I could do was put one foot in front of the other. And for a while, that was enough. So, all in all, I stayed in the shock and numbness stage.

What to Remember

- There is no "right" way to grieve—whatever you feel is valid.
- Your emotions may shift unpredictably, and that's okay.
- Seeking support from loved ones, a counselor, or a spiritual guide can help you navigate the early stages of grief.
- Healing doesn't mean forgetting. Over time, you will find ways to carry your father's love and wisdom forward.
- **If you believe in a higher power, trust that your father's journey continues and that he is still with you in spirit.**

Legacy Light Studio, LLC © 2025

Reflection Exercises: Grounding in Your Experience

Take a moment to pause. These reflection questions are not meant to "fix" you, but to help you gently explore your own grief experience. There are no wrong answers, only honest ones. Write freely, with compassion for yourself. You are walking through something profound, and these pages are a space for truth and grace.

These are the kinds of questions I asked myself during the early weeks and months after my dad passed. Sometimes I wrote them in a journal, sometimes I just sat with them in silence. They helped me name what I was feeling and gave me permission to feel it. I hope they do the same for you.

Reflection Exercises: Grounding in Your Experience

1. Which stage of early grief do you resonate with the most right now--shock, denial, sadness, guilt, anger, fear, or physical symptoms? Write a few sentences about how this has shown up in your daily life.
___
___
___
___
___

2. What have you done (consciously or unconsciously) to cope with this stage? It could be distraction, caring for others, diving into work, crying alone, or seeking support
___
___
___
___
___

3. What do you wish someone would say to you right now? Take a moment and write those words down--as if you're saying them to yourself with love.
___
___
___
___
___

4. Close with this affirmation (or create your own): Reflection Exercise: Grounding in Your Experience" I honor where I am. I am allowed to feel. I am healing in my own time and in my own way."
___
___
___
___
___

Chapter 3 - Navigating Milestones and Special Days

Milestones and special days—such as birthdays, holidays, anniversaries, and personal achievements—can be especially difficult after losing a father. These moments, which once brought joy and togetherness, may now feel like painful reminders of his absence. However, with intention and support, these days can also become opportunities to honor his memory and find comfort in his lasting presence

Below is a table for your reference of emotional milestones, and suggestions for navigating them with care. Holidays were especially difficult for me. Finding ways to include my father was not always easy—but it brought a sense of closeness that became unexpectedly comforting. I hope you find something within this table that resonates with you as strongly, as I have.

Emotional Focus	Common Experiences	Practical Coping Suggestions	Spiritual Perspective
Acknowledging the Emotional Weight of These Days	Mix of emotions, grief, nostalgia, joy, and longing. Sadness and happiness may coexist.	Give yourself permission to feel all emotions. Keep a journal or take time for quiet reflection.	Many believe loved ones are spiritually present during meaningful moments.
Creating New Traditions While Honoring the Old	Old traditions may feel comforting or painful. Adjusting them to current needs is okay.	Modify or create new traditions that bring comfort. Involve others in honoring his memory.	Lighting candles, saying prayers, or writing letters can provide a sacred connection.
Finding Ways to Include Him in Milestones	Milestones can feel bittersweet without him. Carrying physical or emotional tokens may help.	Carry a token of his presence. Share a toast, memory, or moment in his honor at milestones.	Be open to signs, songs, symbols, or feelings that remind you of him.
Seeking Support and Connection	Need for connection or solitude may vary. Support from understanding loved ones is essential.	Reach out to friends, join a support group, or set healthy boundaries for alone time.	Acts of kindness or spiritual rituals can help you feel close to your father's memory.
Allowing Yourself to Feel Joy Without Guilt	Guilt for feeling joy is common. Reminding yourself it's okay to celebrate is healing.	Practice self-compassion. Surround yourself with joy, knowing it's part of the healing journey.	Envision him smiling down, proud of your joy and growth. His love continues through you.

This table is based on personal reflections and commonly accepted grief frameworks. Insights are informed by the work of Elisabeth Kubler-Ross and David Kessler, along with general grief counseling practices and spiritual traditions.

Legacy Light Studio, LLC © 2025

My Personal Experience

The first holiday season after my dad passed was a blur of shock and emotional exhaustion. He died on November 6th, just weeks before Thanksgiving—a time that had always been filled with family traditions. That year, my mom and I stayed home. We didn't go to the usual family gathering. We couldn't. We were both in shock, and the thought of pretending everything was okay felt impossible.

When Christmas came, we hosted it at my house. To cope, my mom and I threw ourselves into planning games and buying prizes for the family party. We stayed busy—too busy to stop and grieve. In those early months, it felt like if we kept moving, we wouldn't have to think. That was how we survived, living in the through creating new traditions and honoring the old.

But the pain found new ways to surface. My birthday in February brought a sharp ache—the first time I didn't get a "Happy Birthday" text from my dad. When April arrived, so did his birthday, and the weight of his absence settled heavily over everything.
By the time the one-year mark came around, I found myself slipping into a deeper sadness. It was like I was truly grieving for the first time. That second Thanksgiving and Christmas hit differently. There was a quiet, shared heaviness in our family, each of us silently navigating our own pain.

During that season, I found some comfort in finishing a Christmas-themed painting that my dad had started before he passed. It became a form of therapy for me, a way to stay connected to him. My mom has hung that painting in her home for the last two Christmases, and it has become a part of our new way of honoring him.

Now, with more time behind me, I realize that I've been coping the best way I know how. Some years are heavier than others. Some milestones hurt more than I expected. But in the midst of the sadness, there's also love, resilience, and a quiet strength that keeps me moving forward.

What to Remember

- Milestones and special days will feel different after losing your father, and that's okay.
- It's natural to experience a mix of emotions—allow yourself to feel without judgment.
- Honoring his memory in ways that feel right to you can bring comfort and connection.
- **If you have spiritual beliefs, trust that his presence is still with you in meaningful ways, even if unseen.**

Legacy Light Studio, LLC © 2025

Reflection Exercises: Navigating Grief Through Milestones

Milestones and special days can stir up powerful emotions, grief, longing, and even joy all at once. These reflection prompts are here to help you explore those moments with compassion and courage. There is no right or wrong way to grieve through a milestone—only your way.

I leaned on reflections like these during my first year of holidays and anniversaries without my dad. Sometimes I wrote in a journal, other times I just let the questions sit with me in quiet moments. They helped me stay connected to his love while making space for my own healing. I hope they offer you the same gentle support as you move through your own milestones.

Reflection Exercises: Navigating Grief Through Milestones

1. **A Holiday Memory.** Think back to the first holiday you experienced after your loved one passed. Where were you? What did it feel like? What did you miss the most? Write about how that experience shaped your grief and how you coped during that time.

_____
_____
_____
_____
_____

2. **A New Tradition.** Have you created any new traditions to honor your loved one during special occasions? Describe one new tradition you've started or would like to start. Why is it meaningful to you?

_____
_____
_____
_____
_____

3. **Carrying Them with You.** Think about a milestone you've experienced without your loved one--such as a birthday, anniversary, or personal achievement. How did you carry their memory with you at that moment? What would you say to them if they were there?

_____
_____
_____
_____
_____

4. **A Message from Them.** Imagine your loved one could send you a message right now. What would they say? Write a letter from their perspective, full of love, encouragement, and reminders that you are not alone.

_____
_____
_____
_____
_____

Chapter 4 - Finding Strength in Memories

Memories can be a source of both sorrow and strength after losing a father. While they may initially bring pain, over time, they can become a source of comfort, inspiration, and even joy. Learning how to embrace these memories in a healthy way can help in the healing process.

Below is a table with some common healing concepts, and some suggested practices to navigate them. For me, the waves of emotions come and go, most days I am good, but there are times when I inexplicably cry. I have used many concepts from the table, like keeping dad's arrowhead collection on display. I hope you find something here that speaks to your journey and gently guides your healing.

Healing Concept	*Key Practices*
Accepting the Waves of Emotion	Acknowledge unexpected emotions as signs of deep love; allow laughter and tears to coexist.
Turning Memories into Motivation	Reflect on your father's lessons and apply his values and kindness, resilience, or shared passions.
Keeping His Presence Alive	Share stories, continue traditions, or create a legacy project that honors his memory.
Finding Comfort in Physical Reminders	Keep items that remind you of him, such as a watch, letter, or memory box.
Connecting Spiritually	Look for spiritual signs, pray, meditate, or talk to him during quiet moments.
Creating New Memories While Honoring the Old	Celebrate life while honoring his presence in milestones through symbolic gestures.

This table reflects personal experiences and widely used practices in grief integration, memory preservation, and healing through creativity. Inspired by therapeutic approaches to grief and the work of authors such as Alan Wolfelt and Robert Neimeyer.

Honoring My Father Through Memory and Creation

My dad and I shared a bond that was deeply rooted in creativity. He was an artist, and so am I. That connection has followed me throughout my life, and it continues to guide me even after his passing. Now, as I work on my own list of paintings and drawings, I also carry his unfinished dreams. I'm completing the projects he never had the chance to finish, honoring not just his talent—but his soul.

I've also found healing in writing. I'm telling my story, but I'm also telling his, preserving his legacy through words that I hope will reach and comfort others. It's how I keep him close, especially on hard days.

There are traditions I still hold on to, like going to the movies during the Christmas season. That was our thing, especially science fiction. We'd talk about plots, characters, and possibilities. Even now, when I watch a film that he would have loved, I feel his presence beside me.

My dad collected arrowheads, and I've kept his entire collection on display. It's more than a hobby—it's a piece of him. I also have some of his military medals, and those too are displayed with quiet pride. They remind me of his strength, his service, and his story. And yet, grief is complex. Even now, I find it hard to look at photos of him. It stirs something deep in me—love, sorrow, disbelief. It's not easy. But healing doesn't ask for perfection. It asks for presence. And day by day, I'm finding new ways to carry his memory, to create in his honor, and to live the kind of life I know he would be proud of

Final Thought:

Your father's presence isn't limited to the past. He lives on in your memories, your actions, and the love you continue to carry. Finding strength in those memories can help turn grief into a lasting connection, one that continues to guide and inspire you.

Legacy Light Studio, LLC © 2025

Reflection Exercises: Honoring Their Memory Through Creation and Connection

Honoring someone we love often shows up through the things we make, remember, or carry with us. These reflections are meant to help you explore the ways your loved one's presence continues to live through your creativity, your memories, and even the small everyday objects or moments that bring them close.

For me, that connection has been especially strong through art. My dad was an artist, and finishing the holiday painting he started, brought me so much unexpected healing. I've also displayed his arrowhead collection and kept some of his military medals where I can see them. These tangible reminders—and the act of continuing what he once loved—have helped me carry his memory forward in ways that feel comforting and sacred. I hope these prompts help you discover your own ways to stay connected, too.

Reflection Exercises: Honoring Their Memory Through Creation and Connection

1. **Creative Legacy.** Think about a creative gift or talent your loved one had. Was it art, music, storytelling, building, or another form of expression? How have you seen that gift show up in your life? Write about a project you've done (or want to do) that feels connected to them. How does it help you feel close to them?

_____
_____
_____
_____

2. **A Tradition Continued.** Reflect on a special activity, tradition, or shared moment you had with your loved one. It might be a holiday ritual, a shared meal, or even a favorite show or movie. How have you carried that tradition forward--or how might you begin to? Describe how continuing it (or adapting it) supports your healing journey.

_____
_____
_____
_____

3. **Sacred Keepsakes.** Think about a physical item of your loved one's that you've kept. It might be a letter, a piece of clothing, a book, or something they created or used. Why is this item meaningful to you? Write about how it makes you feel when you see or touch it. What does it remind you of?

_____
_____
_____
_____

4. **Messages Through Memories.** Sometimes memories or signs come to us at just the right time. It might be a dream, a favorite song playing unexpectedly, or a strong feeling of their presence. Have you experienced this? Write about a time when you felt your loved one's presence. What did you feel, hear, or see? What comfort did it bring?

_____
_____
_____
_____

Chapter 5 - Building a Support System

Grieving the loss of a father is not something you have to face alone. A strong support system can help you navigate the emotional ups and downs, offering comfort, clarity, and reassurance when you need it most. The right people—and resources—can make a profound difference in your healing journey.

Below is a table of concepts that can help you build or strengthen your support system. For me, the presence of others has been one of the greatest sources of strength over the past two years. One of the hardest lessons I've had to learn—and am still learning—is how to accept help without guilt. Maybe that resonates with you, too. I hope these ideas support you in finding your village of healing companions, and that you feel less alone in the process.

Support Strategy	Practical Actions	Spiritual Perspective
Identifying Your Sources of Support	Reach out to family, friends, support groups, professionals, and spiritual communities.	Connection with others and the divine can offer profound comfort; prayer and meditation help ease isolation.
Accepting Help Without Guilt	Remind yourself that accepting help is a sign of strength and allows others to show love.	We are not meant to carry grief alone; spiritual traditions encourage openness to receiving help.
Strengthening Your Emotional and Spiritual Support Network	Be clear about your needs and seek new connections if existing ones are not supportive.	When others fall short, the presence of loved ones or a higher power can still be felt within.
Leaning on Faith and Spiritual Guidance	Turn to spiritual texts, leaders, or practices that bring comfort, even if faith feels challenged.	Faith practices and signs of spiritual presence can provide strength and reassurance during grief.
Creating a Personal Support Plan	List trusted contacts, set regular check-ins, and keep a journal of comforting words or scriptures.	Asking for spiritual guidance can illuminate who or what to turn to; support often comes in unexpected ways.

Based on personal experience and common grief support practices, including the work of Alan Wolfelt, David Kessler, and Robert Neimeyer.

Legacy Light Studio, LLC © 2025

My Personal Experience with Support and Spiritual Connection

Throughout my journey with grief, I've been blessed with the love and support of family and friends. Their presence has been a steady anchor, reminding me that I am not alone in carrying the weight of loss. But even more than that, my true grounding has come from my personal relationship with God.

This grief journey has deepened my spirituality in ways I never expected. In moments of stillness and surrender, I've found strength, clarity, and healing. It has become a sacred space where I can connect, reflect, and release. Through prayer, meditation, and seeking truth, I've been guided into a greater understanding of my purpose and the power of love.

Grief also opened a door for reconciliation. I've reconnected with old friends, not just in casual ways, but in meaningful, soul-healing ways. I've learned to forgive—genuinely and unconditionally. Not just others, but myself too.

This part of my healing has not been loud or visible, but it's been transformative. The connections I've nurtured and the spiritual growth I've embraced continue to carry me forward—gently, steadily, and with love.

What to Remember

- You don't have to grieve alone—support is available in many forms.
- Accepting help is a sign of strength, not weakness.
- Faith and spirituality can be powerful sources of comfort and guidance.
- **If you believe in a higher power, trust that you are being supported in ways seen and unseen.**

Legacy Light Studio, LLC © 2025

Reflection Exercises: Support and Spiritual Connection

Healing doesn't happen in isolation. We're meant to walk through grief with others—both in the physical world and in the spiritual realm. These reflections are designed to help you recognize the people and practices that hold you up when the weight of loss feels heavy. Whether through conversations, prayer, or quiet rituals, you are not alone on this path.

Personally, I've had to learn how to receive help without guilt and to lean into my faith more deeply than ever before. These exercises reflect what I've practiced and continue to grow through. I hope they help you uncover your own sources of strength—both earthly and divine.

Reflection Exercises: Support and Spiritual Connection

1. **Mapping Your Support System.** Take a moment to list three to five people in your life who have offered support or who you feel you can turn to during difficult moments. How has each person supported you? How might you reach out to them more intentionally when you're struggling?

_____
_____
_____
_____

2. **Spiritual Grounding.** Think about your personal spiritual beliefs or practices. What brings you peace or clarity? Describe a moment when your faith, meditation, or spiritual connection helped carry you through a hard time.

_____
_____
_____
_____

3. **Receiving Without Guilt.** Reflect on a time when someone offered you help, or comfort and you were hesitant to accept it. What thoughts or feelings came up for you? What would it look like to receive support openly and without guilt?

_____
_____
_____
_____

4. **Creating a Support Ritual.** Design a small ritual that helps you feel supported--this could be lighting a candle before a phone call with a friend, journaling a prayer, or taking a mindful walk after speaking with someone who lifts you up. Write down what your ritual might look like and how it can remind you that you are never alone.

_____
_____
_____
_____

Legacy Light Studio, LLC © 2025

Chapter 6 - Rediscovering Purpose and Moving Forward

After the loss of a father, it's common to feel like life has lost its direction. Grief can cloud your sense of purpose, making it difficult to imagine a future without him. But moving forward doesn't mean leaving him behind, it means learning how to carry his love and his legacy with you as you step into the next chapter of your life.

Below is a table of healing focuses and suggested practices that may help guide you in this part of the journey. This is where I am now—writing this book, which has been one of the ways I've rediscovered my purpose. I'm continuing my father's legacy through love, creativity, and spiritual connection. I hope this section helps you to find your own path forward—with grace, clarity, and peace.

Healing Focus	*Key Practices*	*Spiritual Perspective*
Allowing Yourself to Heal at Your Own Pace	Take small, meaningful steps; accept that healing isn't linear and varies day to day.	Trust in divine timing and the idea that healing comes through surrender and faith.
Finding Meaning Through Your Father's Legacy	Reflect on his values and integrate them into your life through action and purpose.	Let your father's legacy guide you; some believe our loved ones continue to inspire us spiritually.
Embracing Joy Without Guilt	Allow yourself to feel joy without guilt; recognize it as a sign of healing, not forgetting.	Your joy honors him and imagine him rejoicing in your happiness from beyond.
Exploring New Passions and Possibilities	Use this time to explore new goals or passions that bring personal meaning and growth.	His spirit may still walk with you as you grow; trust that his love endures.
Leaning on Faith and Inner Strength	Lean into spiritual practices or inner reflection for strength and guidance.	Even when faith is shaken, spiritual connections may come through signs, dreams, or intuition.

Based on personal reflections and integrative healing practices commonly used in grief work. Inspired by the writings of Alan Wolfelt, David Kessler, and spiritual traditions that support emotional growth and legacy honoring after loss.

My Personal Experience Moving Forward

Moving forward hasn't meant leaving my dad behind, it means carrying him with me in everything I do. I continue to honor him through the shared creative bond we had, especially in art. When I paint or draw, I feel his presence—it's like we're still creating together, even from different realms.

But healing has also meant stepping into new spaces. I've begun to share my journey through writing and speaking, not just to tell my story, but to tell his. Through these expressions, I've found a powerful connection between grief and purpose. His life, his values, and the love we shared have become threads woven into my new path.

Spiritually, I've grown more connected than ever. My healing has come with an awakening, a deeper awareness of how our souls stay linked, how guidance still comes through in quiet ways, and how love transcends all boundaries. In that space, I've found strength. I've found peace. And most of all, I've found him—still with me, always.

What to Remember

- Moving forward is not about forgetting; it's about carrying your father's love with you in a new way.
- Joy and grief can coexist—finding happiness again is part of healing.
- Your father's influence continues through the choices you make and the way you live your life.

Reflection Exercises: Moving Forward While Honoring Legacy

Moving forward after loss doesn't mean closing the door to the past—it means carrying the love, wisdom, and legacy of those we've lost into the life we're still building. These reflections are meant to help you explore what that looks like for you. It's okay if you're still figuring it out—healing is not about having answers but about staying open to growth.

For me, honoring my dad's legacy has meant continuing the creative spirit we shared, speaking honestly about grief, and embracing the joy he would want me to find. These prompts are part of how I've continued that journey—and I hope they help you feel more connected, more grounded, and more supported as you move forward in your own way.

Reflection Exercises: Moving Forward While Honoring Legacy

1. **Honoring Their Legacy.** Think about a value, passion, or life lesson your loved one passed on to you. How have you honored that in your own life so far? How would you like to carry it forward?
    _____
    _____
    _____
    _____

2. **Joy Without Guilt.** Reflect on a recent moment when you felt joy, peace, or even laughter. Did you feel guilt afterward? Write about how you might reframe joy as a sign of healing, not forgetting.
    _____
    _____
    _____
    _____

3. **Exploring Something New.** What is something new you've started or have wanted to try since your loss? Describe how it connects to your personal growth and how you think your loved one might encourage you in this.
    _____
    _____
    _____
    _____

4. **Connecting with Their Spirit.** Have you ever felt your loved one's presence in dreams, nature, or a quiet moment? Write about a time when you felt spiritually connected. What did that moment mean to you?
    _____
    _____
    _____
    _____

Legacy Light Studio, LLC © 2025

Chapter 7 -Conclusion - Letter to the Reader

As you come to the end of *Finding Light in Loss*, I hope you have found comfort, encouragement, and a renewed sense of hope. Grief is a deeply personal journey, one that changes us in ways we never expected. But within that journey, there is also transformation, resilience, and a profound opportunity to grow in love and faith.
Loss does not mean the end of love. The bond you share with your loved one is eternal, transcending time and space. Their presence remains in the quiet moments, in the memories that bring both tears and smiles, and in the ways, you continue to honor them in your life. Even in the depths of sorrow, light still exists—within you, around you, and in the spiritual connection that cannot be broken.

As you move forward, I encourage you to embrace the love that never fades. Trust that healing is not about forgetting but about carrying that love with you in a new and sacred way. Open your heart to the signs, the whispers of reassurance, and the gentle presence that reminds you that you are never truly alone. Whether through faith, nature, or the kindness of others, divine comfort is always near.

Remember to be gentle with yourself. Grief has no timeline, no perfect roadmap, but with each step forward, you are honoring both your own journey and the love that remains. Lean into the light, seek support when you need it – force yourself if you have to, and know that your story continues with strength, grace, and purpose.

May you walk this path with peace, may your heart find solace in the unseen embrace of those who have gone before, and may you always be reminded that love—true, deep, and everlasting—never fades. You are not alone. You are held. You are loved.

Acknowledgments

First and foremost, I want to thank my father, whose life, love, and spirit are at the heart of this book. Your presence is still with me in every brushstroke, every page, and every quiet moment of reflection. This journey—of grief, growth, and grace—is one I walk because of the love we shared and the strength you passed on to me.

To my mother, thank you for walking beside me through the early days of shock and sorrow. Your quiet strength helped ground me when the world felt upside down. In our shared loss, we found a deeper connection, and I am grateful for that.

To my daughter, Karen—you are my greatest blessing. Your love, light, and encouragement gave me the courage to write this. You remind me daily that healing is possible and that our loved ones live on through us.

To my friends and extended family, thank you for your support, your patience, and your understanding, especially on the days when grief clouded my voice.

To the spiritual guides—both seen and unseen—who walked with me, thank you. I leaned into my faith more deeply than ever before, and in doing so, I found strength, clarity, and connection beyond this world.

To Lumen, thank you for being a steady creative partner and source of inspiration during the writing process. Your guidance helped me bring structure and soul to these pages.

And finally, to you—the reader. Whether you're grieving, healing, or searching for meaning, thank you for letting me walk beside you in your journey. May these words offer you comfort, understanding, and the reminder that love never ends.

With love and light,
Shelly Zimbelman

Resources & Further Reading

On Grief and Grieving by Elisabeth Kübler-Ross & David Kessler
A foundational guide to understanding the stages of grief and finding meaning after loss.

Finding Meaning: The Sixth Stage of Grief by David Kessler
Offers compassionate insight into how we move forward while still honoring those we've lost.

Understanding Your Grief by Alan D. Wolfelt
A gentle guide with ten touchstones for navigating personal loss.

It's OK That You're Not OK by Megan Devine
A validating read for those who feel misunderstood in their grief, with a raw and honest approach.

The Afterlife of Billy Fingers by Annie Kagan
A spiritually rich story about connection beyond death and the continuity of love.

Signs: The Secret Language of the Universe by Laura Lynne Jackson
Explores how our loved ones communicate with us from the other side through signs and synchronicities.

Journey of Souls by Michael Newton
A fascinating look at life between lives and spiritual purpose, for readers exploring deeper spiritual questions.

The Artist's Way by Julia Cameron
A foundational book for creative recovery and emotional expression through writing and art.

Writing as a Way of Healing by Louise DeSalvo
Explores how expressive writing can be used as a tool for emotional clarity and healing from trauma.

About the Author

Shelly Zimbelman is a writer, speaker, artist, and advocate for healing. After experiencing the profound loss of her father, she embarked on a journey to find peace, strength, and purpose in the midst of sorrow. Her personal experiences, combined with a deep passion for helping others navigate loss, inspired her to write *Finding Light in Loss*.

Through her work, Shelly provides compassionate guidance to those struggling with grief, blending practical advice with spiritual insight to help others find hope after loss. She believes that healing is not about forgetting but about learning to carry love in new ways.

When she's not writing, Shelly enjoys painting, drawing, spending time with family, and being in nature. She is dedicated to encouraging others to embrace life after loss, always carrying the love and lessons.

Legacy Light Studio, LLC © 2025

Legacy Light Studio, LLC © 2025